W9-BNU-606

j
791.4572
BEA

Beatty, Scott,
1969-

Superman, the
animated series
guide.

$9.99

DATE			

GATES PUBLIC LIBRARY
1605 BUFFALO RD
ROCHESTER NY 14624

05/04/2004

BAKER & TAYLOR

SUPERMAN

THE ANIMATED SERIES GUIDE

LONDON, NEW YORK, TORONTO,
MELBOURNE, MUNICH, AND DELHI

Editor Alastair Dougall
Designer Robert Perry
Art Director Mark Richards
Publishing Manager Cynthia O'Neill Collins
Category Publisher Alex Kirkham
Production Nicola Torode

First American Edition, 2003
03 04 05 10 9 8 7 6 5 4 3 2 1

Published in the United States by DK Publishing, Inc.,
375 Hudson Street, New York, New York 10014

Copyright © 2003 by DC Comics

SUPERMAN and all related characters, names, and indicia
are trademarks of DC Comics © 2003. All rights reserved.

Page layout copyright © 2003 Dorling Kindersley Limited

All rights reserved under International and Pan-American Copyright Conventions. No part of this publication may be
reproduced, stored in a retrieval system, or transmitted in any form or by any means, electronic, mechanical,
photocopying, recording, or otherwise, without the prior written permission of the copyright owner.
Published in Great Britain by Dorling Kindersley Limited.

DK Publishing, Inc. offers special discounts for bulk purchases for sales promotions or premiums. Specific, large-quantity
needs can be met with special editions, including personalized covers, excerpts of existing guides, and corporate imprints.
For more information, contact Special Markets Department, DK Publishing, Inc., 375 Hudson Street, New York, NY 10014.
Fax: 800-600-9098.

Library of Congress Cataloging-in-Publication Data

Beatty, Scott, 1969-
  Superman, the animated series guide / by Scott Beatty.-- 1st American
ed.
    p. cm. -- (DC animated series guides)
Includes index.
  ISBN 0-7894-9584-8 (hardcover)
  1. Superman (Television program : 1996-2000) I. Title. II. Series.
PN1992.77.S833B43 2003
791.45'72--dc21

2003000918

Reproduced by Media Development and Printing, UK
Printed and bound in Italy by L.E.G.O.

Visit DC Comics online at www.dccomics.com or at keyword DC Comics on America Online.

see our complete product line at
www.dk.com

SUPERMAN

THE ANIMATED SERIES GUIDE

Written by Scott Beatty
Superman created by Jerry Siegel and Joe Shuster

DK

CONTENTS

WELCOME TO METROPOLIS

Oh, the sights you'll see! This is the heart of Superman's world, a teeming urban center unlike any other city on Earth. From the offices of the *Daily Planet* newspaper to the underworld of Suicide Slum, the Man of Steel defends Metropolis from villainy.

And the threats are many. You might witness power-hungry Lex Luthor plotting to control all of Metropolis. Or spy cruel cyborg Metallo destroying Stryker's Island with robotic glee! Or watch as Darkseid's invaders teleport right into the heart of downtown!

But standing in their way is the Last Son of Krypton. Whether battling supervillains intent on destroying Metropolis or flying to the stars to save Earth from certain doom, this Man of Tomorrow fights a never-ending battle for truth, justice, and freedom for all.

As you walk the streets of Metropolis, you might catch a glimpse of him if you look up in the sky.

It's not a bird or plane.

It's Superman!

KRYPTON'S LAST SON

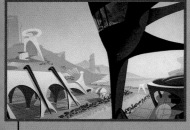

When still a baby, Superman was rocketed to Earth from the dying planet Krypton. Before that, the Man of Steel was simply Kal-El, only son of Jor-El and Lara. Jor-El was Krypton's greatest scientist. He alone knew that internal pressures within the planet's core would cause Krypton to explode!

BRAINIAC'S BETRAYAL

Jor-El tried to warn the people of their fate. However, the members of Krypton's High Council believed the lies of super-computer Brainiac. It soothed their fears and turned them against Jor-El! Brainiac escaped from Krypton, while Jor-El raced home to save his son.

SUPERMAN'S LEGACY is a glowing orb (left), which contains all that remains of Kryptonian knowledge and culture.

KRYPTON'S FINEST

Kal-El's parents were among Krypton's best and brightest citizens. Jor-El's scientific achievements included discovery of the Phantom Zone, which imprisoned Krypton's criminals.

SUPER DATA

• Kal-El's rocket carried the Phantom Zone Projector and a device that would later reveal his true origins.

• Kal-El's mother, Lara, was an historian who chronicled the rise of Krypton's civilization and its destruction.

THE HOUSE OF EL featured a spectacular view of Krypton's landscape. It was set apart from other Kryptonian dwellings and offered Jor-El an opportunity to conduct his scientific studies without interruption.

KAL-EL'S TINY ROCKET was a prototype for larger spaceships Jor-El hoped to build. If there had been time, these ships could have ferried Kryptonians to safety.

DEATH OF A PLANET

As the planet crumbled around them, Jor-El arranged baby Kal-El's departure from their doomed world. The couple bid a tearful farewell to the Last Son of Krypton.

THE KENTS

J onathan and Martha Kent of Smallville, Kansas were in just the right place when baby Kal-El's rocket came crashing to Earth. The Last Son of Krypton was an answer to the childless couple's prayers. The Kents raised him as their own son. But Clark Kent was no ordinary boy…

THE PORCH of the Kent homestead has seen many good heart-to-heart talks between Clark and his folks.

CLARK DIDN'T KNOW the truth behind his miraculous abilities until the Kents showed him the Kryptonian rocket. Then they told Clark the amazing story of how he arrived on Earth.

THE GREATEST GIFT

Jor-El and Lara, Clark's Kryptonian parents, couldn't have picked a better home for their son. The Kents brought him up to be honest and true, and taught him that *helping* people can be the greatest gift of all.

SUPER DATA

- Semi-retired, the Kents still work on the farm.

- They are guardians to Kara In-Ze of Argo—Supergirl!

CALLING BIG BLUE

The Kents have seen some mighty strange things as parents to super-children! When Kara was stricken with a deadly virus from her frozen homeworld, the Kents called Superman for help!

HAPPY FAMILY

When they aren't off saving the world, Superman and Supergirl both know that home, warm hugs, and great family meals are just a super-speed flight away.

SMALLVILLE HIGH SCHOOL was Clark's home away from home for several years. There, he had a teenage crush on his pretty classmate, Lana Lang.

A PROBLEM SHARED

Sometimes even *superpowers* aren't enough to solve a problem. The Kents have always shared their troubles with each another... often over Ma Kent's homemade apple pie.

SUPERMAN

He is the greatest hero in the world. The Man of Steel has devoted his life to fighting a neverending battle for the causes of freedom and liberty. Blessed with extraordinary superpowers under the rays of Earth's yellow sun, the Last Son of Krypton fearlessly defends his adopted planet Earth from the forces of evil everywhere!

Thanks to his solar-energized muscles, Superman can toss a truck with ease!

BULLETPROOF

Kal-El's skin was toughened under Krypton's heavier gravity. Under Earth's yellow sun, Superman is practically invulnerable. Bullets bounce harmlessly off his super-tough skin!

SUPERMAN'S heat vision can melt the hardest metal. X-ray vision allows him to see through nearly every substance except lead.

FREEZING BREATH pours from Superman's mouth and stops criminals cold! The Man of Steel can also hold his breath underwater for hours.

An invisible, solar-charged aura around Superman's skin protects him from injury and makes his costume indestructible too!

SAVING LIVES is Superman's top priority. He can snatch people from danger and fly them to safety in seconds!

UP, UP...

...and *AWAY*! Earth's lighter gravity allows Superman to leap tall buildings in a single bound.

SUPER DATA

• Superman's secret base is the Fortress of Solitude, a Kryptonian hideaway in the Arctic circle.

• Kryptonite is the radioactive remnants of Planet Krypton, pieces of which fell to Earth as meteorites.

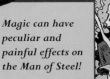

Magic can have peculiar and painful effects on the Man of Steel!

WEAKNESSES

Superman may be bulletproof, but he can still be hurt. Magic can stagger him, while green kryptonite takes away his powers. Prolonged exposure to the radioactive rock could kill him.

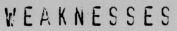

CLARK KENT

Meek and mild-mannered Clark Kent isn't just a reporter for the great Metropolitan newspaper the *Daily Planet*. He's also the alter ego of the Man of Steel! The small-town boy from Smallville watches over the city of Metropolis as both a crusading reporter and as the world's greatest hero—Superman!

PRESS MAN

One of the *Daily Planet*'s top reporters, Clark is on the front line when major news is breaking. Of course, Superman is never far behind if an exciting story needs a helping hand!

SUPER DATA

• By slicking back his hair and donning a pair of glasses, Clark conceals his identity as Superman!

• Clark usually wears his Superman costume beneath his business suit.

FRIENDLY RIVALRY exists between Clark and fellow reporter Lois Lane. Lois tries to out-scoop Clark with Superman stories, unaware that the Man of Steel is closer than she thinks!

LANA LANG

Before Lois Lane stole Clark (and Superman's) heart, his first love was Lana Lang. Clark was later shocked to learn that his red-haired former flame was now a famous fashion designer dating Lex Luthor!

FAMILY OUTINGS in Metropolis are happy times for the Kents. Ma and Pa like nothing better than going out to dinner with son Clark and niece Kara.

THE SECRET REVEALED!

Clark has always taken care to guard his secret identity. When trouble starts, he usually slips away to a vacant broom closet for a quick-change into his Superman costume. On a few occasions, Clark's secret has come dangerously close to being exposed!

BRAD WILLIAMS, former Smallville High bully, guessed that Clark was really Superman. Clark fooled him thanks to a stand-in Superman: *Batman in disguise!*

THE DAILY PLANET

No other newspaper is as famous as the *Daily Planet*. It has won every major award for its hard-hitting investigative reporting. The Daily Planet Building, also home to the 24-hour Planet News Broadcasting, is topped by a golden globe, shining like a beacon of truth over Metropolis.

PERRY WHITE

Perry is Managing Editor of the *Daily Planet*. One of the newspaper's most successful reporters, he now runs the day-to-day business of the publication and approves every story it publishes.

PERRY'S TEMPER is legendary, especially when Jimmy Olsen calls him "Chief." But his bark is far worse than his bite.

JIMMY OLSEN

Photographer Jimmy grew up on the mean streets of Metropolis's Suicide Slum. He's a good kid with a knack for finding (and getting into) trouble. Jimmy doesn't know that Clark Kent is also his best pal, Superman!

RON TROUPE is a recent addition to the editorial staff. Like his fellow journalists, Ron has a real nose for news and frequently chronicles the exciting adventures of Superman.

ANGELA CHEN is the *Daily Planet*'s gossip columnist. She's also the host of *Metropolis Today*, an entertainment show televised on Planet News Broadcasting.

WHAT A TEAM!

The *Daily Planet* has only the best and brightest journalists. With Jimmy Olsen providing the photos, Clark Kent and Lois Lane write all the news that's fit to print!

SUPER DATA

• With Clark Kent on staff, the **Planet** always scoops its rivals with the latest news on Superman.

• Green Lantern (Kyle Rayner) used to work in the newspaper's art department.

LOIS LANE

Troubleshooting reporter Lois Lane was renowned for risking life and limb to get a story. So when her hard-won scoop on a dockside gun-smuggling racket was dropped for weird reports of a flying "guardian angel" patrolling the skies of Metropolis, she was determined to find out the truth!

Lois Lane has won many awards for her investigative writing— even the Pulitzer Prize. Other newspapers have courted her, but Lois has no plans to leave her beloved *Daily Planet*.

LOIS STRIKES a pose with Clark at a Metropolis charity function. Jimmy's camera never lies: Lois and Clark make a great couple!

DANGER GIRL

Lois knows how to take care of herself! Her father, U.S. Army General Sam Lane, taught her martial arts, handy skills when Lois goes undercover to follow up on a sinister scoop!

SUPER DATA

• When Metropolis's guardian angel saved Lois from a berserk LexCorp battlesuit, she thanked her hero by introducing him to the public as as Superman.

• Lois suspects that Clark Kent might be Superman, but she has yet to uncover convincing proof!

EVERLASTING LOVE

When Superman first met Lois Lane, it was love at first sight for the man of Steel. The same was true for Clark Kent! Over time, Lois and Superman have grown closer. Clark, meanwhile, longs for the day when he can reveal his secret identity to Lois.

Superman's greatest fear is that Lois might be hurt by one of his vengeful enemies!

LOIS'S RELATIONSHIP with Superman may put her in harm's way, but it also brings her exclusive stories concerning the Man of Steel, such as when he shrank to micro-size!

KNOCKOUT!

Lois Lane never backs away from a fight. Realizing her reporting partner, Clark Kent, wasn't behaving normally, she socked him in the jaw and unmasked an imposter! Superman, meanwhile, just slipped away so that the *real* Clark could return.

SUPERGIRL

Superman's secret weapon is an astonishing teenage girl named Kara. He rescued her from the icy planet Argo, where she was the sole survivor of her people. And like Superman himself, Kara possesses amazing superpowers under Earth's sun—making her a true Supergirl!

Supergirl designed this stylish costume herself!

ARGO'S ICY END

Krypton's sister planet Argo was also devastated when Krypton exploded. The shock wave from Krypton's destruction hurled Argo out of its natural orbit. Moving away from its red sun, Argo soon froze to death.

SLEEPING Kara was discovered in cryogenic freeze on Argo's icy surface as Superman searched Krypton's solar system for familiar signs of life.

SMALLVILLE is Kara's new home on Earth. She lives there with the Kents, who encourage their "niece" Kara to conceal her growing superpowers.

SMALL TOWN GIRL

Superman wanted Kara to become accustomed to Earth before revealing her super-abilities. But Kara felt she was ready for action. She designed her own costume and flew to Metropolis. Unfortunately, she flew right into trouble!

KANTO the assassin was one of Darkseid's evil minions. He underestimated Supergirl and was amazed when the blade of his knife shattered on her steely skin!

POWER GIRL

Supergirl's abilities are similar to those of Superman. She is super-strong, can fly at super-speeds and is invulnerable to injury. She also has X-ray and heat vision.

SUPER DATA

• Supergirl's best friend is Batgirl.

• Superman refers to Supergirl as his "cousin."

• Unlike Superman, Supergirl is not affected by kryptonite radiation.

JUSTICE LEAGUE

The Man of Steel isn't alone in his never-ending fight to uphold truth and justice. Among his closest friends are some of the world's greatest super heroes, such as Batman and Wonder Woman. Like them, Superman is a member of the Justice League of America, the titanic team sworn to defend Earth and the cause of freedom everywhere with its super-powered might!

THE JLA in action: Green Lantern subdues the Parasite; Wonder Woman knocks Metallo for a loop!

MARTIAN MANHUNTER J'onn J'onzz of the JLA employs Martian science to heal a mangled Man of Steel.

THE JLA

The super-hero team's lineup includes (clockwise from left) The Flash, The Martian Manhunter, Hawkgirl, Superman, Wonder Woman, Green Lantern, and Batman.

SUPER DATA

- Wonder Woman makes villains 'fess up with her Lasso of Truth.

- Steel's main weapon is a super-powerful sledgehammer.

- The JLA's base is the Watchtower satellite.

STEEL

Former LexCorp engineer John Henry Irons adapted his designs for police battle armor to create a suit for himself. He aids Superman as Steel!

Superman and Batman disagree at times, but they're both totally devoted to fighting crime!

BATMAN

Metropolis and Gotham City are near neighbors, so it was only a matter of time before the Man of Steel and the Dark Knight joined forces to defend their respective cities from organized villainy.

METROPOLIS

Some call it the "Big Apricot." Others know it as "The City of Tomorrow." This ultra-modern urban landscape, with its mile-high gleaming skyscrapers and elevated roadways, is the most exciting place on the planet. Metropolis leads the world in science, arts, and industry. But its greatest claim to fame is that Metropolis is the city Superman calls *home*.

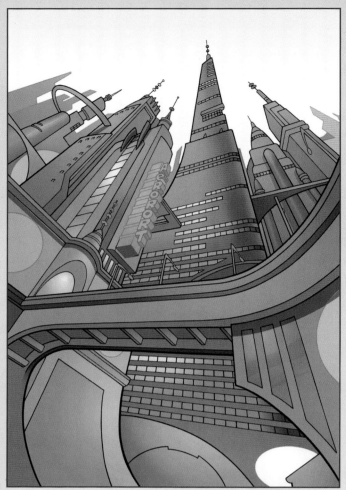

LEXCORP TOWER is the tallest building in Metropolis. Like a would-be ruler, Lex Luthor gazes down upon the city from a penthouse office on the uppermost floor.

S.T.A.R. LABS

Based in Metropolis, the Scientific and Technological Advanced Research Laboratories is a high-tech think tank. At S.T.A.R. Labs, many of the world's top minds work on new inventions to benefit mankind.

PROFESSOR EMIL HAMILTON is perhaps the most brilliant man in Metropolis. This kindly scientist invents many of the incredible gadgets used by the Man of Steel, and also designed his anti-kryptonite suit.

SUPER DATA

• Several miles offshore from Metropolis is Stryker's Island Maximum Security Penitentiary.

• Metropolis was once the beachhead for Darkseid's planned invasion of Earth!

LAW AND ORDER

When Superman is away, the task of keeping the peace in the city falls to the Metropolis Special Crimes Unit. Lt. Maggie Sawyer (right), a tough-as-nails cop, is head of the S.C.U. Sadly, Maggie's former partner Dan Turpin (left) died defending Metropolis from Darkseid's invading forces.

INTERGANG

The Intergang, led by Bruno "Ugly" Mannheim, is a coalition of mobsters bent on taking over Metropolis. Mannheim is aided by Darkseid, who provides Intergang with weapons and technology from Apokolips.

LEX LUTHOR

Before Superman arrived, Lex Luthor was the most powerful man in Metropolis. His corrupt business empire LexCorp still touches the lives of every citizen. To the public, Luthor is simply a successful businessman. But to Superman, power-hungry Luthor is the most dangerous man on Earth!

DESTROYER OF LIVES

Ruthless and lacking all conscience, Luthor won't hesitate to sacrifice others to achieve his sinister ends. He turned criminal John Corben into the cyborg Metallo. Compared to other employees, Corben got off lightly!

AAAGGHHH!

Master of disguise Multi-Face is one of the supervillains hired by Luthor to assassinate Superman.

EVIL PLANS

LexCorp profits by manufacturing weapons and other lethal technology. Lex Luthor sometimes eliminates his competition personally. Other times, he employs costumed supervillains to carry out his dirty deeds.

- Before Superman came to Metropolis, Luthor plotted to win Lois's heart by hook or crook!

- Unlike Superman, Luthor has no superpowers, but he is both a scientific and a criminal genius.

SUPERMAN'S DEFEAT is Lex Luthor's number one goal! He has spent billions of dollars trying to eliminate the Man of Steel. But Luthor is always careful to cover his tracks.

MERCY GRAVES is Luthor's chauffeur and bodyguard. She is totally loyal to Luthor and would willingly give her life to protect him from his enemies.

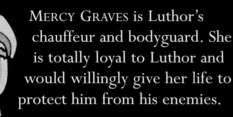

ALWAYS FOILED

Superman continually reminds Luthor that he's watching him. This constant supervision has prevented many of Luthor's criminal undertakings. It has also made Luthor even more determined to rid himself of Superman!

DARKSEID

Apokolips is a world of evil far, far away. Its ruler is the dread lord Darkseid, a tyrant who will stop at nothing to rule the universe! And first on his list of cosmic conquests is a small but significant planet—Earth, adopted world of Superman!

SHZAAK!

OMEGA BEAMS are destructive rays, which Darkseid emits from his eyes. These rays can disintegrate foes or teleport them across vast distances.

APOKOLIPS

There is no hope on Apokolips. The planet is nothing but a giant factory churning out weapons of mass devastation! Flying Parademons patrol the scarred landscape while Lowlies toil in the shadows of huge stone statues dedicated to Darkseid!

DESAAD

Darkseid's top torturer is the devilish Desaad. He is the chief inquisitor of Apokolips and is responsible for interrogating all of Darkseid's captives. Here, a helpless Jimmy Olsen suffers in Desaad's dungeon laboratory.

GRANNY GOODNESS doesn't live up to her name! In her horrible orphanage, Granny trains helpless young girls to be Female Furies loyal to Darkseid.

PARADEMONS are vicious, genetically engineered monsters who act as Darkseid's living air force.

SUPER DATA

• The New Gods, from the peace-loving planet New Genesis, are sworn enemies of Darkseid.

• Darkseid's good son Orion helped Superman to thwart his father's invasion of Earth.

• Darkseid can even withstand Superman's mighty blows!

KALIBAK

Darkseid's youngest son, the ogre Kalibak the Cruel, is eager to earn his fiendish father's approval. Kalibak once traveled to Earth in order to annihilate Superman and finally gain Darkseid's acceptance.

METALLO

Beneath John Corben's metal skin beats a heart of kryptonite! Corben was hired by Lex Luthor to steal a LexCorp battlesuit as part of a plan to test Superman's powers. When Corben, now in prison, became fatally ill, Luthor offered him the chance of a new lease on life with an indestructible robot body!

COVERED in "Metallo," an alloy developed by LexCorp, Corben lived on. However, he could not feel anything with his metal skin and was driven to destruction!

KILLER HEART

Metallo's mechanical body is powered by a chunk of pure kryptonite. This element, harmless to humans, is the only substance that can kill Superman with its lethal radiation.

SUPER DATA

• Metallo's super-strong exoskeleton is powerless without his kryptonite heart.

• Corben hates Luthor for turning him into Metallo.

• Metallo's cyborg punches can knock Superman senseless!

HOW TO BEAT METALLO

Defeating Metallo isn't easy! Superman can't risk getting close to Metallo's kryptonite heart. He must fight from a distance, aiming to separate Corben from his kryptonite power source.

SUPER METALLO

Superman found some serious competition when Superior-Man came to Metropolis! But appearances can be deceiving. The Man of Steel soon discovered that Superior-Man was really a brainwashed Metallo!

LUTHOR'S PLAN all along was to create a supervillain who could beat Superman! It was Luthor himself who infected Corben with the deadly illness. Corben had to agree to a life inside an unfeeling robotic body—or die!

BRAINIAC

If not for Brainiac, there wouldn't be a Superman! Brainiac was a sophisticated super-computer built many years ago on Krypton. The planet's governing council based all of its major decisions on Brainiac's advice. Unfortunately, he advised them to ignore Jor-El's warning that Krypton would soon explode!

The linked discs on Brainiac's forehead reflect his original Kryptonian design.

ENEMIES

To escape Krypton, Brainiac downloaded himself onto an orbiting satellite. He arrived on Earth as an orb packed with dangerous information.

LESS THAN HUMAN

Brainiac is a ruthless machine. After taking Lex Luthor hostage, he impersonated the Metropolis mogul with a computer simulation. Meanwhile, Brainiac forced the real Luthor to help him build an android body to inhabit!

SH-LAKK!

SUPER DATA

• Brainiac can overtake and overwhelm any computer system.

• Except for Superman's Fortress of Solitude, Brainiac's programming is all that remains of Kryptonian technology.

INVASION PLOT

When Brainiac arrived on Earth, Superman learned that he, too, was from Krypton. Inside Brainiac's massive starship, the Man of Steel uncovered Brainiac's secret intent to dominate Kal-El's adopted world!

SUPERMAN'S FATHER Jor-El realized too late that Brainiac was evil. Jor-El could not stop Brainiac from dooming Krypton! Kal-El, however, would not allow the computer tyrant to achieve his goal of conquering the Earth.

BRAINIAC'S BODY can be destroyed by Superman's searing heat vision, but his artificial intelligence lives on. He always finds a way to download his computerized consciousness and escape to battle the Man of Steel another day!

Rudy Jones is no longer human.

PARASITE

Petty thief Rudy Jones was a janitor at S.T.A.R. Labs in Metropolis. To pay off gambling debts, Jones tried to steal experimental chemicals from the company. But as he fled from a pursuing Superman, he spilled the toxic liquids on himself. The resulting chemical reaction turned him into a mutated monster: the power-hungry Parasite!

The Parasite absorbs energy through physical contact

SUPER DATA

• Jones must continually feed on bio-energy to survive, or he will weaken and wither.

• When imprisoned at Stryker's Island, the Parasite is kept on a strict "low energy" diet to stop him escaping.

POWER SUCKER

Unknown contents in the S.T.A.R. Labs chemicals transformed Rudy Jones into a creature that feeds on the bio-energy from other living beings. The Parasite's appetite for this power is insatiable!

SUPER HUNGRY

Superman's powers are the Parasite's favorite snack! In his first encounter with the Man of Steel, Jones consumed much of Superman's Kryptonian life-energies. As a result, the Parasite briefly gained many of Superman's powers, including heat vision, super-strength, and the ability to fly!

RAIN-SONG is a psychic healer, a specialist in crystals—and the object of Rudy Jones' obsession. The Parasite believed that he might win her heart by defeating Superman once and for all.

MXY'S POWERS ABSORBED

When the Parasite turned his attention from Superman to Mr. Mxyzptlk, he absorbed Mxy's Fifth-Dimensional magic. The Parasite turned Lois Lane into Darkseid and Jimmy Olsen into Brainiac, and brought a Superman monument to life in Metropolis!

BIZARRO

The creature known as Bizarro is a clone grown from the Man of Steel in a secret mountain laboratory owned by Lex Luthor. At first, Bizarro was identical to Superman. But Kryptonian DNA is difficult to duplicate. Soon the clone mutated into a twisted version of the real Superman—a Monster of Steel!

BIZARRO'S PET, Krypto, shows his devotion Bizarro style—by biting his master!

BIZARRO'S WORLD

Bizarro isn't evil, but he always does the exact opposite of Superman. To keep this duplicate from being a super-threat, the Man of Steel transplanted Bizarro to an uninhabited alien world where he can do no harm.

BIZARRO INHERITED Superman's affection for Lois Lane. But the imperfect clone's clumsy attempts to impress Lois with his super-strength frightened her instead!

CRUSH ON LOIS

Lois is the one person Bizarro would never hurt. But when Mr. Mxyzptlk convinced the confused clone that Lois and Superman were making fun of him, he flew straight to Earth to get even!

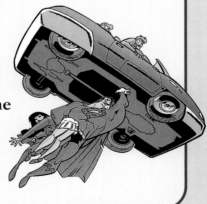

SUPER DATA

• Luthor's top geneticist, Dr. Teng, was responsible for cloning Bizarro.

• Bizarro took Krypto from the Interplanetary Zoo housed in Superman's Fortress of Solitude.

BIZARRO LOIS is an imperfect clone of Lois Lane created by Bizarro using Luthor's damaged cloning equipment. They live together on Bizarro World.

LIVEWIRE

Leslie Willis was the rudest radio star in Metropolis, filling her broadcasts with rants against Superman. But the Man of Steel gave her the jolt of her life! As a thunderstorm raged at a concert promoting her radio show, a bolt of lightning passed through Superman's body and turned Leslie into Livewire, a being of pure electrical energy!

SUDDEN APPEARANCES are easy when you can surf on microwaves! Livewire beams in via a fireman's cellular phone.

HIGH-VOLTAGE VILLAIN

Livewire is composed entirely of living electricity. She can control electric power in all its forms, making her a high-powered villain who can zap Superman silly!

BRAINIAC

Livewire caused a shock when she saved the world! When Brainiac was about to press a button that would detonate every atomic bomb on Earth, Livewire used her powers to short-circuit the nuclear nightmare!

SUPER DATA

• Livewire drains her powers with each use and must recharge.

• Livewire once teamed with Bat-rogues Poison Ivy and Harley Quinn to fight Supergirl and Batgirl. But, currently, she has given up her electrifyingly evil ways.

LEX LUTHOR helped Livewire after Superman shorted out her powers. Luthor provided just enough energy to recharge Livewire's anger against Superman.

STICKING TO LOIS like static cling, Livewire goads Superman into coming to Lois's rescue. The former "shock jock" loves the media attention drawn to her buzzing battles with the Man of Steel!

SAVING SUPES

Livewire helped save Earth a second time when she teamed with Superman in repelling the armies of Darkseid! But her greatest act of heroism was jolting Superman back to life after a massive power overload stopped his heart!

Jax-Ur & Mala

Superman thought he was planet Krypton's sole survivor—until he met Jax-Ur and Mala. Superman accidentally set free these cruel Kryptonian villains using the Phantom Zone Projector, which he found in the rocket that had first brought him to Earth.

Jax-Ur's right eye was replaced by a Kryptonian cybernetic optical unit.

Jax-Ur

Jax-Ur has reason to hate the son of Jor-El. Before he was sent to the Phantom Zone, Jax led a military coup on Krypton that was squashed by none other than Superman's own father!

TROUBLE MAKERS Jax-Ur and Mala use their newfound superpowers to turn Metropolis into a war zone!

SHRUNKEN to more manageable size by S.T.A.R. Labs, the Kryptonian villains anxiously awaited Earth's justice.

MALA

Don't let her good looks fool you! After pretending to follow Superman's heroic example, Mala attacked Professor Hamilton and used the Phantom Zone Projector to free Jax-Ur!

KRYPTONITE

As Kryptonians, Jax-Ur and Mala are susceptible to kryptonite's deadly rays. Supergirl, however, hails from Argo and is not affected by kryptonite. Tackling the villains without fear of also harming Superman, Supergirl used the green-glowing element to weaken Jax-Ur and Mala.

SUPER DATA

• Superman once traveled through a black hole and discovered the escaped Jax-Ur and Mala ruling a planet on the other side!

BATTLING SUPERGIRL wasn't as easy as Jax-Ur and Mala thought! The Phantom Zone villains locked the Girl of Steel in the sights of their high-tech cannon, but she retaliated with a blast of energy from the Phantom Zone Projector!

39

TOYMAN

Toymaker Winslow Schott Sr. tinkered with trouble when he borrowed money from Intergang to build his factory. Schott ended up dying in prison. Meanwhile, his son—Winslow Schott Jr.—went to an orphanage and toyed with thoughts of revenge on Intergang and its boss, Bruno Mannheim!

Don't open! That Toyman action figure just might be packed with plastic explosive!

PLAYING FOR KEEPS

Schott Jr. blamed Mannheim for the ruin and death of his toymaking father. As the Toyman, Schott Jr. plotted Mannheim's destruction with a plethora of perilous playthings!

ONLY SUPERMAN'S X-ray vision can reveal if a swooning siren is for real… or a deadly doll.

PLAY PALS

Journalists Clark Kent and Lois Lane visited the Toyman in Stryker's Island prison, only to find the diabolical doll-maker every bit as evil as ever!

MINI SUPERMEN

Superman stopped the Toyman killing Bruno Mannheim. But when Schott Jr. couldn't get his evil way, he decided to frame Superman! Miniature Man of Steel action figures soon swarmed all over Metropolis, stealing from children!

Reporter Ron Troupe's niece Tasha knew that there was something strange inside her Superman toy!

TICK
TICK
TICK
TICK

KABOOM!!

WHOOM!!!

IF ALL ELSE FAILS...

...the Toyman will blow up his own toy-box to get away! Just when Superman thinks he's nabbed Schott, the grinning gamester explodes an identical decoy by remote control!

SUPER DATA

• The Toyman has no love for children *whatsoever*!

• He once created a beautiful, life-size doll which escaped his control and became top fashion model Darci Mason!

LOBO

The alien known as Lobo is the last Czarnian... because he wiped out his entire planet! Now he roams the spaceways as a bounty hunter. But the "Main Man"—as Lobo calls himself—will work for free if the job involves a brawl and a rip-roarin' good time!

LOBO ZOOMS from galaxy to galaxy on his customized space cycle, the Hog.

THE MAIN MAN

Lobo traveled to Earth when a being called the Preserver contracted him to net the Last Son of Krypton for a private zoo! Lobo brought his bounty back after a tremendous fight, but found himself caged as well!

SUPER DATA

• Lobo is so tough he's virtually indestructible.

• He can travel through space without a personal air supply.

• Lobo takes victims dead or alive. He's not fussy.

Lobo thanked Superman in his own special way for busting him out of the Preserver's zoo—by punching the Man of Steel! Of course, Lobo had told Superman that he would attack Earth if the hero didn't help him!

Lobo doesn't shower often. His body odor is as offensive as his manners.

BIG TIME LOSER

The Main Man likes a good game of cards as much as he likes a fight. He plays for high stakes: he once forged a deed to planet Earth then lost it in an interstellar poker game! Luckily, Superman won Earth back and Lobo had to pay off his gambling debts waiting tables.

BOUNTY HUNTER

Lobo is the most successful bounty hunter in the galaxy. He's mean and he's dangerous. And don't even think about short-changing the Main Man when it comes to his finder's fee!

MR. MXYZPTLK

Mxyzptlk is an imp from from the fabulous Fifth Dimension, a weird world where everyone wields wacky powers! But there's no one like Superman in Mxy's realm, so, every 90 days, this trickster travels to Earth just to play pranks jokes on his favorite foe, the Man of Steel!

MISS GSPTLSNZ is proof that opposites attract. Tall, stunningly beautiful Gspy wishes her itty-bitty boyfriend would give up taunting Superman.

KRYPTO was baby Kal-El's puppy on planet Krypton. In a cruel practical joke, Mxyzptlk traveled back in time and stole Krypto.

OUTSMARTING MXY

If Superman can trick this tiny trickster into speaking or writing his name backwards, then Mxy is banished back to his home dimension for no less than 90 days. But Mxy never allows himself to be defeated the same way *twice*!

44

SUPERBOY

Fed up with being beaten by Superman, Mxy picked a fight with the *Teen* of Steel, Superboy! Traveling back in time, Mxy tried to convince Superboy to leave Earth, creating a bleak future in which Jimmy Olsen was wheelchair-bound and Lois had died!

MAGICALLY DELICIOUS

The Parasite laughed at Mxy's warning to leave Superman alone. In fact, the energy-consuming villain munched some of Mxy's magical powers and made a mutated Perry White think he was the monstrous ape King Kong!

POOOOF!

KLTPZYXM! Superman sends Mxy back where he came from. But the imp always returns to bewilder the Man of Steel.

MXY'S MAGIC always wears off when he's sent back to his own dimension. His antics are usually harmless, but turning *Daily Planet* Managing Editor Perry White into a rampaging giant can have serious consequences!

SUPER DATA

• Mxy's name is pronounced "Mix-yez-pittle-ick."

• Mxyzptlk loves nothing more than humiliating Superman.

• Unfortunately, Mxy knows that Clark Kent is really the Man of Steel!

GAZETTEER

Angela Chen (voiced by Lauren Tomas)
First appeared in THE LAST SON OF
KRYPTON, Part Two (Episode #2).

Batman (voiced by Kevin Conroy)
First appeared in WORLD'S FINEST, Part
One (Episode #39).

Bizarro (voiced by Tim Daly)
First appeared in IDENTITY CRISIS
(Episode #20).

Brainiac (voiced by Corey Burton)
First appeared in THE LAST SON OF
KRYPTON, Part One (Episode #1).

Bruno Mannheim (voiced by Bruce Weitz)
First appeared in FUN AND GAMES
(Episode #4).

Clark Kent (voiced by Tim Daly)
First appeared (as Kal-El) in THE LAST
SON OF KRYPTON, Part One
(Episode #1).

Dan Turpin (voiced by Joe Bologna)
First appeared in TOOLS OF THE TRADE
(Episode #12).

Darkseid (voiced by Michael Ironside)
First appeared in TOOLS OF THE TRADE
(Episode #12).

Emil Hamilton (voiced by Victor Brandy)
First appeared in A LITTLE PIECE OF
HOME ((Episode #5).

The Flash (voiced by Charlie Schlatter)
First appeared in SPEED DEMONS
(Episode #22).

Jax-Ur (voiced by Ron Perlman)
First appeared in BLASTS FROM THE

PAST, Part One (Episode #14).
Jimmy Olsen (voiced by David Kaufman)
First appeared in THE LAST SON OF
KRYPTON, Part Two (Episode #2).

Jonathan Kent (voiced by Mike Farrell)
First appeared in THE LAST SON OF
KRYPTON, Part Two (Episode #2).

Jor-El (voiced by Christopher McDonald)
First appeared in THE LAST SON OF
KRYPTON, Part One (Episode #1).

Kalibak (voiced by Michael Dorn)
First appeared in FATHER'S DAY
(Episode #28).

Lana Lang (teen voiced by Kelly Schmidt;
adult voiced by Joely Fisher)
Teenaged Lana first appeared in THE LAST
SON OF KRYPTON, Part Two (Episode
#2); the adult Lana first appeared in MY
GIRL (Episode #10).

Lex Luthor (voiced by Clancy Brown)
First appeared in THE LAST SON OF
KRYPTON, Part Two (Episode #2).

Lara (voiced by Finola Hughes)
First appeared in THE LAST SON OF
KRYPTON, Part One (Episode #1).

Livewire (voices by Lori Petty)
First appeared in LIVEWIRE
(Episode #18).

Lobo (voiced by Brad Garrett)
First appeared in THE MAIN MAN, Part
One (Episode #8).

Lois Lane (voiced by Dana Delany)
First appeared in THE LAST SON OF
KRYPTON, Part Two (Episode #2).

Maggie Sawyer (voiced by Joanna Cassidy)
First appeared in TOOLS OF THE TRADE
(Episode #12).

Mala (voiced by Leslie Easterbrook and
Sarah Douglas)
First appeared in BLASTS FROM THE
PAST, Part One (Episode #14).
Martha Kent (voiced by Shelly Fabares)

First appeared in THE LAST SON OF
KRYPTON, Part Two (Episode #2).

Mercy Graves (voiced by Lisa Edelstein)
First appeared in A LITTLE PIECE OF
HOME (Episode #5).

Metallo (voiced by Malcolm McDowell)
John Corben first appeared in THE LAST
SON OF KRYPTON, Part Two (Episode
#2). Corben became Metallo in THE WAY
OF ALL FLESH (Episode #6).

Mr. Mxyzptlk (voiced by Gilbert
Gottfried)
First appeared in MXYZPIXILATED
(Episode #21).

Miss Gsptlsnz (voiced by Sandra Bernhard
and Jennifer Hale)
First appeared in MXYZPIXILATED
(Episode #21).

Parasite (voiced by Brion James)
First appeared in FEEDING TIME
(Episode #7).

Perry White (voiced by George Dzundza)
First appeared in THE LAST SON OF
KRYPTON, Part Two (Episode #2).

Ron Troupe (voiced by Dorian
Harewood)
First appeared in THE LAST SON OF
KRYPTON, Part Two (Episode #2).

Steel (voiced by Michael Dorn)
John Henry Irons first appeared in
PROTOTYPE (Episode #31). He became
Steel in HEAVY METAL (Episode #34).

Supergirl (voiced by Nicholle Tom)
First appeared in LITTLE GIRL LOST,
Part One (Episode #37).

Superman (voiced by Tim Daly)
Kal-El first donned the costume of
Superman in THE LAST SON OF
KRYPTON, Part Two (Episode #2).

Toyman (voiced by Bud Cort)
First appeared in FUN AND GAMES
(Episode #4).

INDEX

ACKNOWLEDGMENTS

Dorling Kindersley would like to thank the following DC artists for their contributions to this book:

Christian Alamy; Aluir Amancio; Terry Austin; Terry Beatty; Bret Blevins; Ron Boyd; Rick Burchett; Wayne Faucher; Chris Jones; Min S. Ku; Mike Manley; Andy Merrill; David Michelinie; Joe Staton; Neil Vokes; Stan Woch.

The author would like to gratefully thank:
Steve Korté, Alastair Dougall, Robert Perry, Shaun McLaughlin, Kevin Kiniry, and Jennifer Myskowski.

Dorling Kindersley would like to thank:
Steve Korté and James Gardner at DC Comics; Julia March for editorial assistance.

PLEASE SHARE YOUR THOUGHTS ON THIS BOOK

comments:	comments:
comments:	comments:
comments:	comments:
comments:	comments:
comments:	comments:
comments:	comments: